GOD

VOLUME 2
TWEENS VERSION

FOR TWEEN GIRLS

is in the

DETAILS!

DISCOVERING GOD'S LOVE THROUGH COLOR & DESIGN!

GOD IS IN THE DETAILS -Volume II Tweens Version
Discovering God's Love Through Color & Design

All Scripture quotations, unless otherwise indicated, are taken from the Holy Bible.
All songs and hymns quoted are in the public domain.

Trade Paperback ISBN

Cover design by Harvest Creek Design; cover image by Teresa Granberry
Illustrated by Teresa Granberry & Caitlyn Granberry

Published in the United States.

This book is available at a special quantity discount when purchased in bulk by corporations,
organizations, or special-interest groups.   For more information, please contact
teresa@harvestcreek.net.

LIFE IS EXCITING WHEN GOD IS WITH YOU!

Welcome to *God is in the Details, Volume II.* If you are a young girl (*or simply young-at- heart*) this book is for you. It combines coloring fun with important lessons about God's unconditional love.

It was a real blessing to work on this book with my granddaughter, Caitlyn. She is creative and artistic and many of the drawings were her original ideas.

As you randomly color these pages, I hope you will connect with the Lord through the creativity displayed. Allow His thoughts and ideas to fill your mind while drawing works of art. Y-O-U were one of His masterpieces; let Him inspire masterpieces through you, right here!

Use your imagination, be original, use patterns and colors to express yourself. Some pages will be quick and easy to finish. Other designs are a little more complicated; take your time and enjoy! Flip through the book and work on whatever catches your eye. And most importantly, remember that God is involved in the details of your life.

Teresa Granberry
Harvest Creek Design

TIPS FOR SUCCESS:
Put another sheet of paper behind the page
you are working on - - - to prevent colors bleeding
onto the next design.

Use markers, colored pencils, crayons, gel pens...
or a combination of each one!

Even if the background is blank feel free to add
your own lettering and patterns.

"Gigi" & Caitlyn

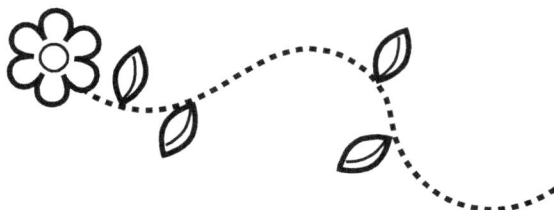

FUN PATTERNS TO FILL YOUR ARTWORK

Solid fill isn't the only way to color your art.
Use the patterns below for ideas to complete the pages of this book.

DOTS

SQUARES

HEARTS

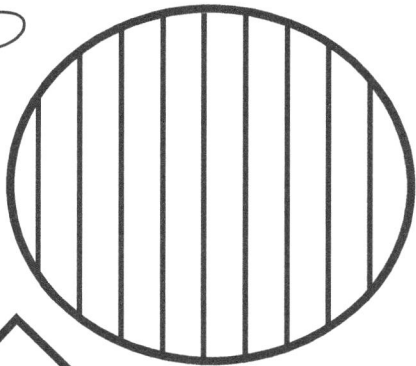

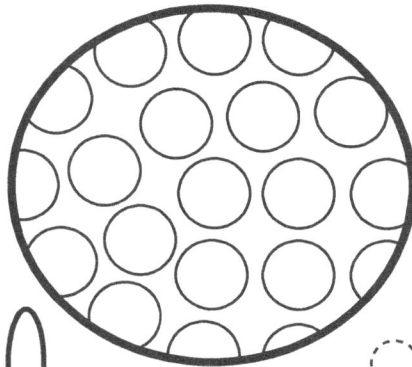

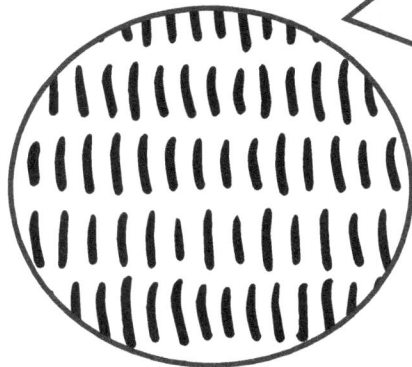

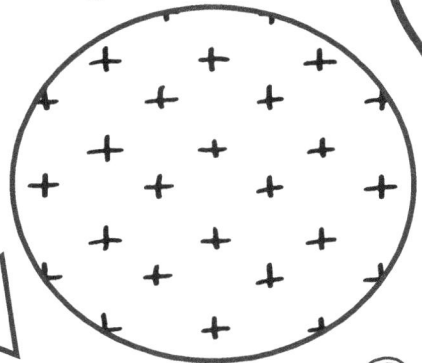

RANDOM LINES

SQUIGGLYS

Congratulations!
You now own a DONUT SHOPPE.
Create your own specialties.

MY DONUT SHOPPE

OPEN

I "DONUT" KNOW WHAT I WOULD DO
WITHOUT JESUS IN MY LIFE!

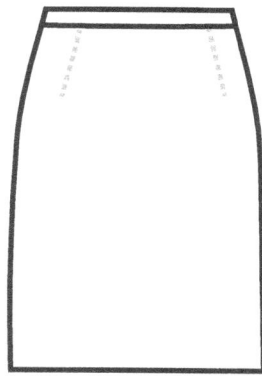

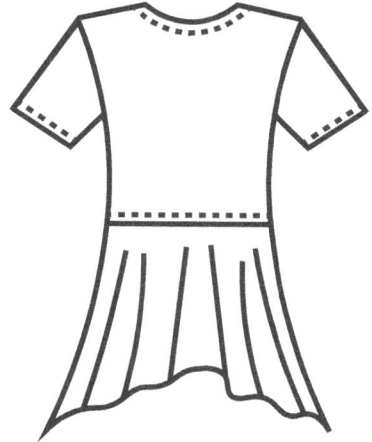

SHE
is clothed with
STRENGTH
and
DIGNITY

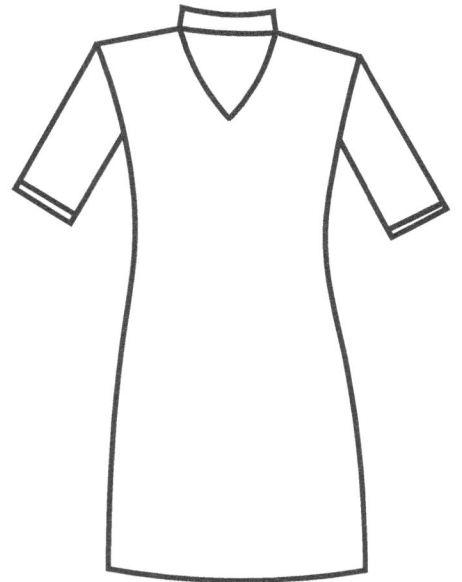

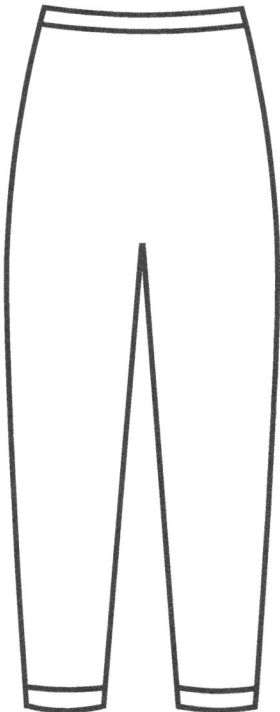

Add buttons, ruffles, collars and other items to decorate this clothing to match your own style.

KEEP CALM...and feed the fish!

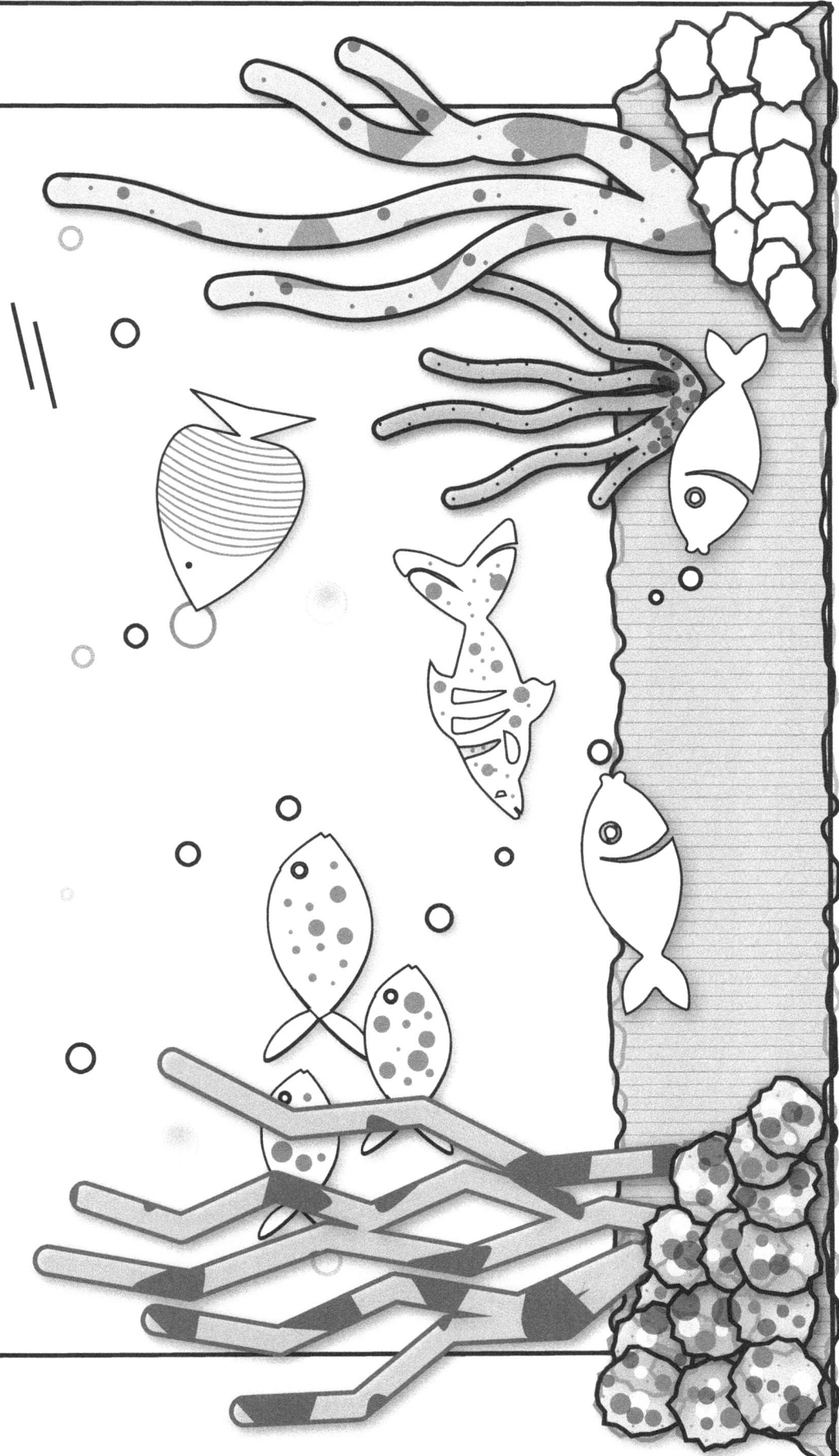

Always Be Kind.

NO MATTER HOW YOU FEEL!

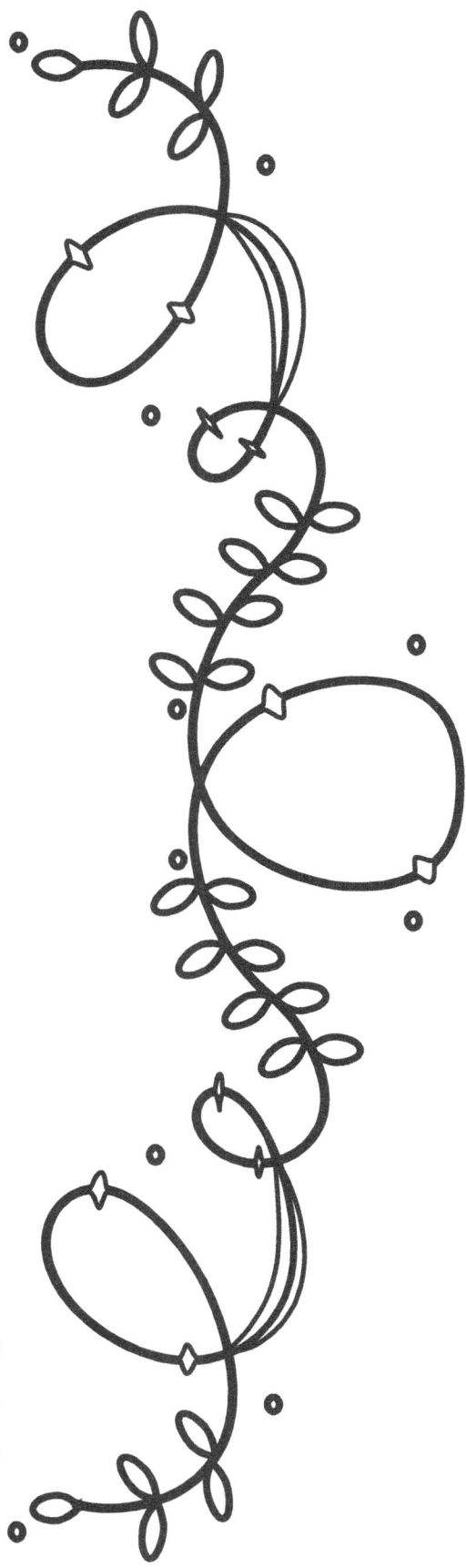

IF SOMEONE NEEDS A FRIEND...

BE 1

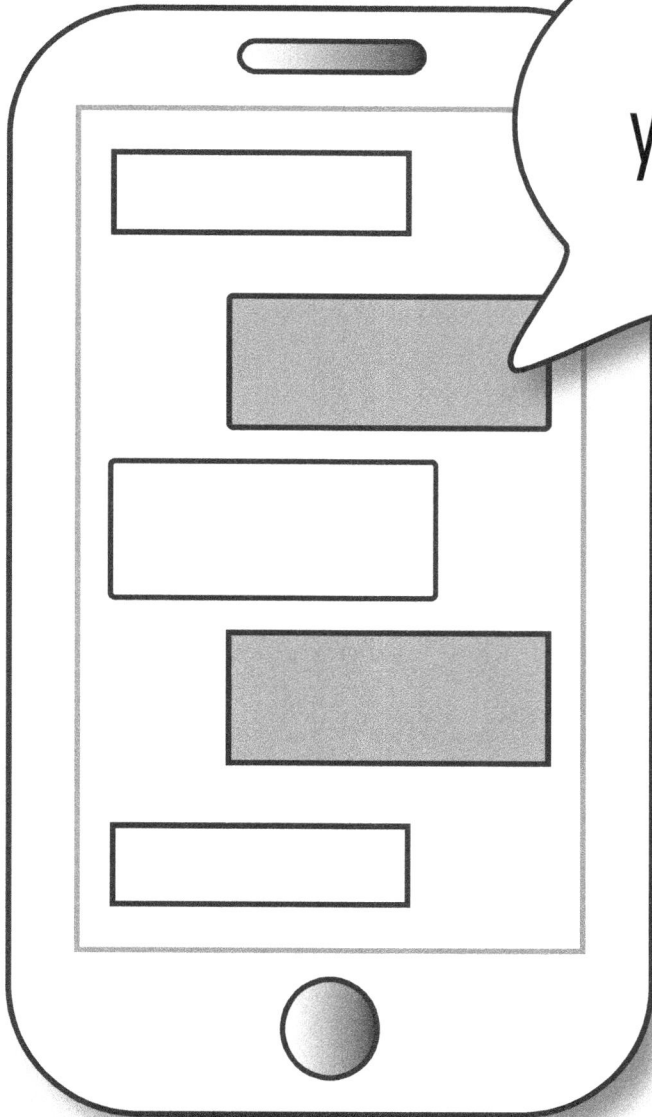

MESSAGES FROM HEAVEN

Faith

You can always trust me!

I created you.
I made you in my own image.
I love you as a parent loves his child.
I will never leave you alone.

Love

Always do for other people everything you want them to do for you.

W I S D O M

GRACE

Sometimes you will cry, because you are sad. But the world is still good because I created it. I understand your pain and soon it will turn to joy.

Never stop praying!

Mercy

FAVOR

Be kind to your parents! They need your support!

I have **BIG PLANS** for Y-O-U!

Believe

The Rainbow is GOD'S PROMISE

I AM LIFTING UP THE NAME OF JESUS

I AM LIFTING UP THE NAME OF JESUS

I AM LIFTING UP THE NAME OF JESUS . . .

Dear God:

   I want to be close to you.   But
sometimes it feels like you are far away.
How can I be with you more?
   Please show me how to make that happen.

Love,

Have you ever wondered

what you were going to become once you're grown?

God's plan for you fits together like a quilt.

Every gift and talent in your life is a piece of His perfect plan.

And each piece forms a beautiful masterpiece.

You are God's work of art!

What are some talents the Lord has given you to

form your "life quilt"? Write them in the squares below.

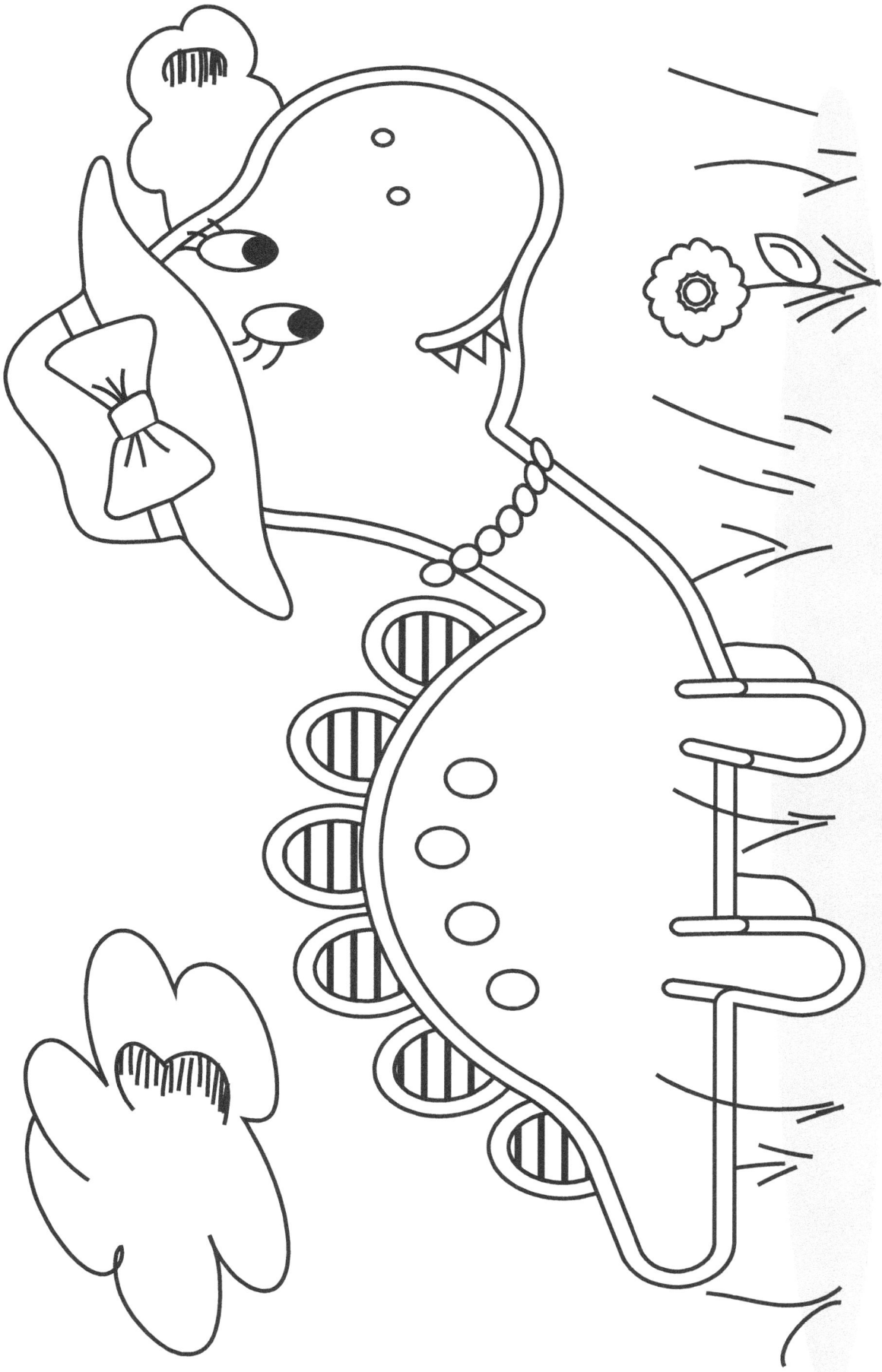

Be DINO-RIFFIC

GOD IS AMAZING!

My Favorite Things

Design your own t-shirt . . . front and back! Choose a fun message to display. Be creative!!

You can do it!

SUPER GIRL!

Never Never Never Give up!

My Purpose

HANG IN THERE!

GOD IS WITH ME!

I am
BEE-utiful
to Jesus!

Where are you going? Draw your destination in the window.
Design the car with your favorite colors.

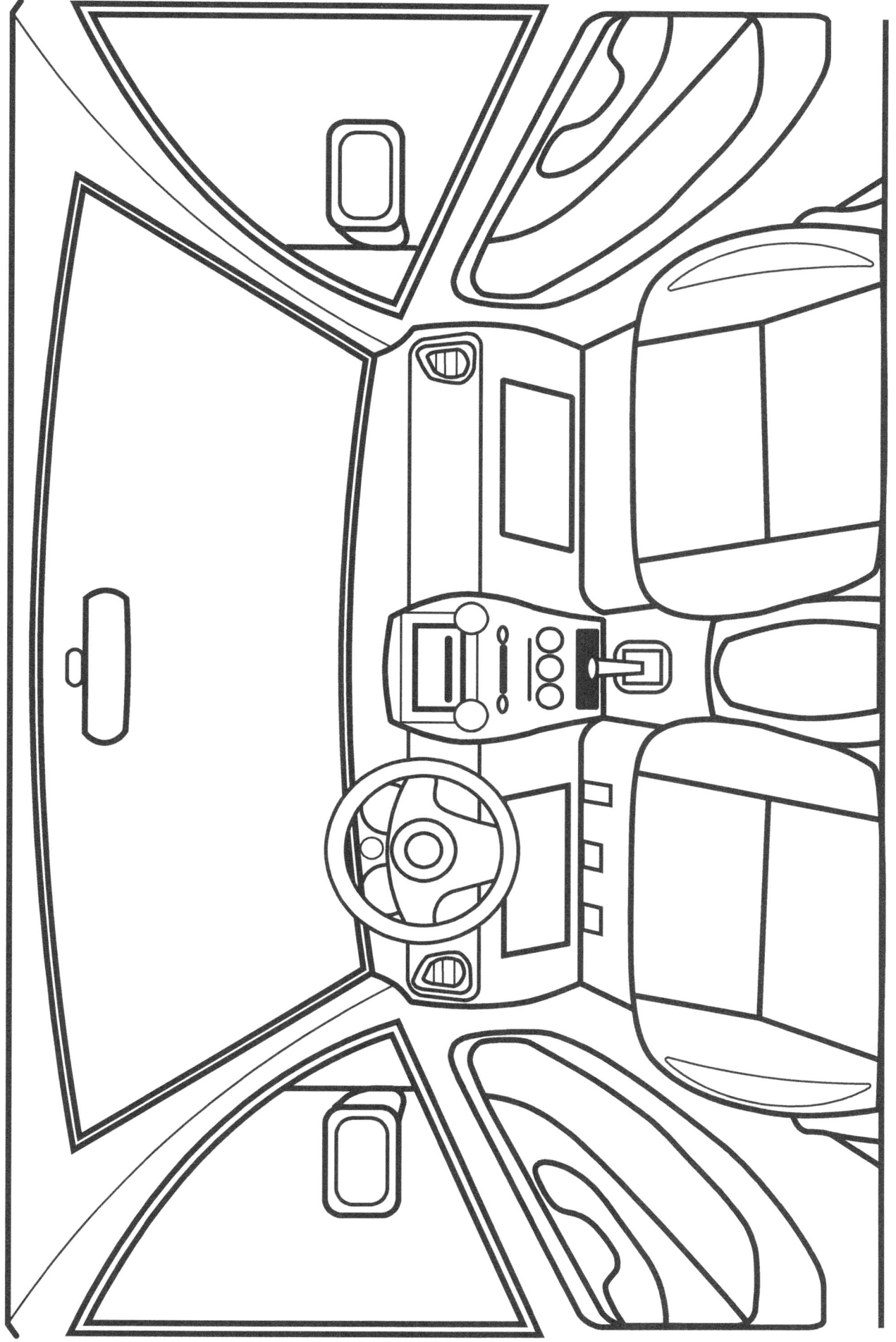

WORDS HAVE

SUPER POWER!

WHOEVER SAID, "STICKS & STONES CAN BREAK MY BONES, BUT WORDS WILL NEVER HURT ME" WAS W-R-O-N-G!! WORDS CAN HURT. WRITE SOME POSITIVE WORDS THAT WILL ENCOURAGE SOMEONE WHEN SPOKEN IN LOVE.

BE
YOUR
OWN
KIND
OF
BEAUTIFUL

God is a SHiELD.
He's got
your back!

FRIENDS THAT I WILL PRAY FOR:

Before You Were Born, I Knew You.

I Love. . .

My Favorite Song:

My Favorite Book:

I am:

My Favorite TV Show:

My Favorite Color:

My Favorite Meal:

Inches Tall

I am a precious jewel
to Jesus! *Isaiah 43:4*

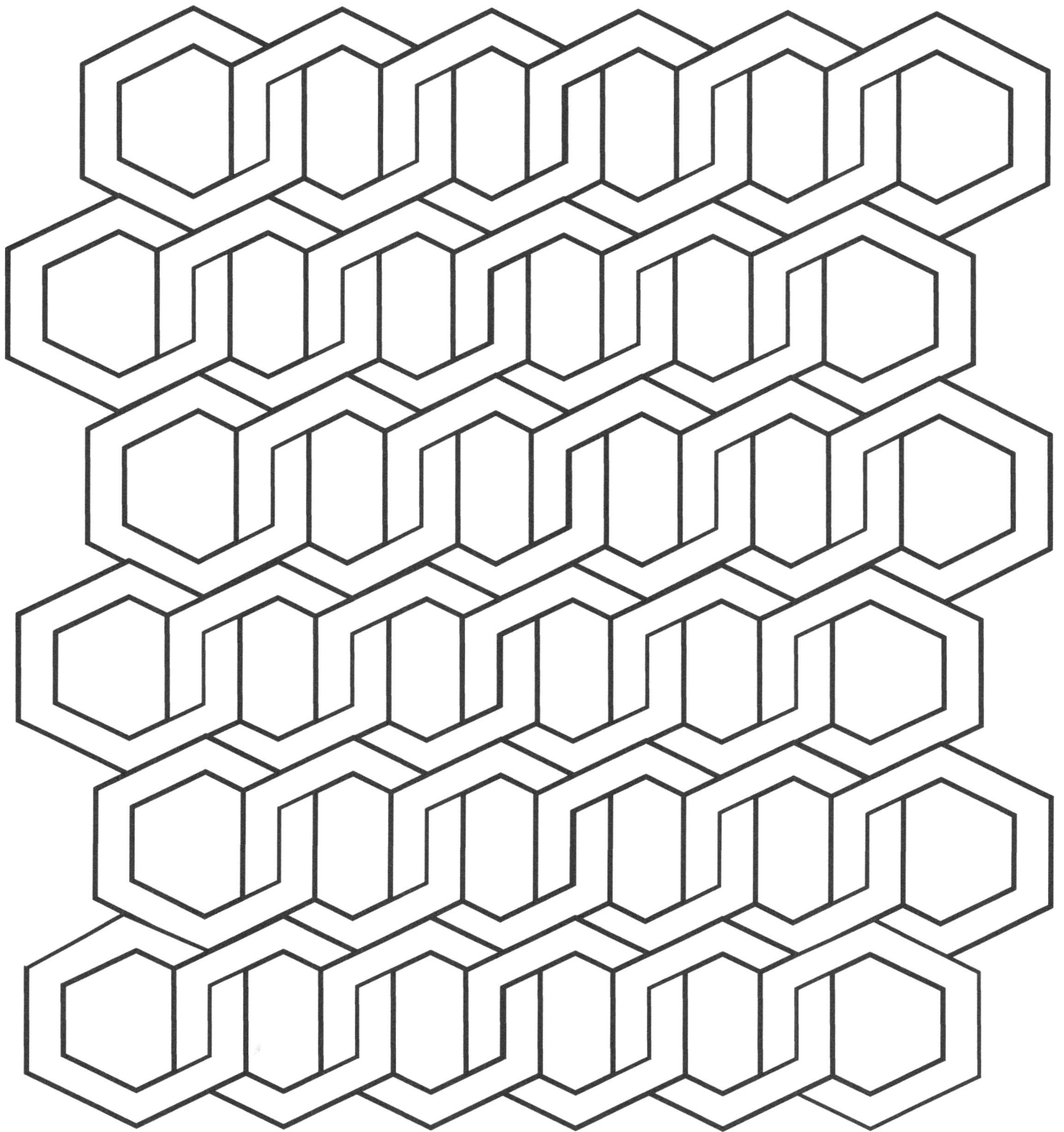

GOD HAS AN AMAZING PLAN
JUST FOR ME.

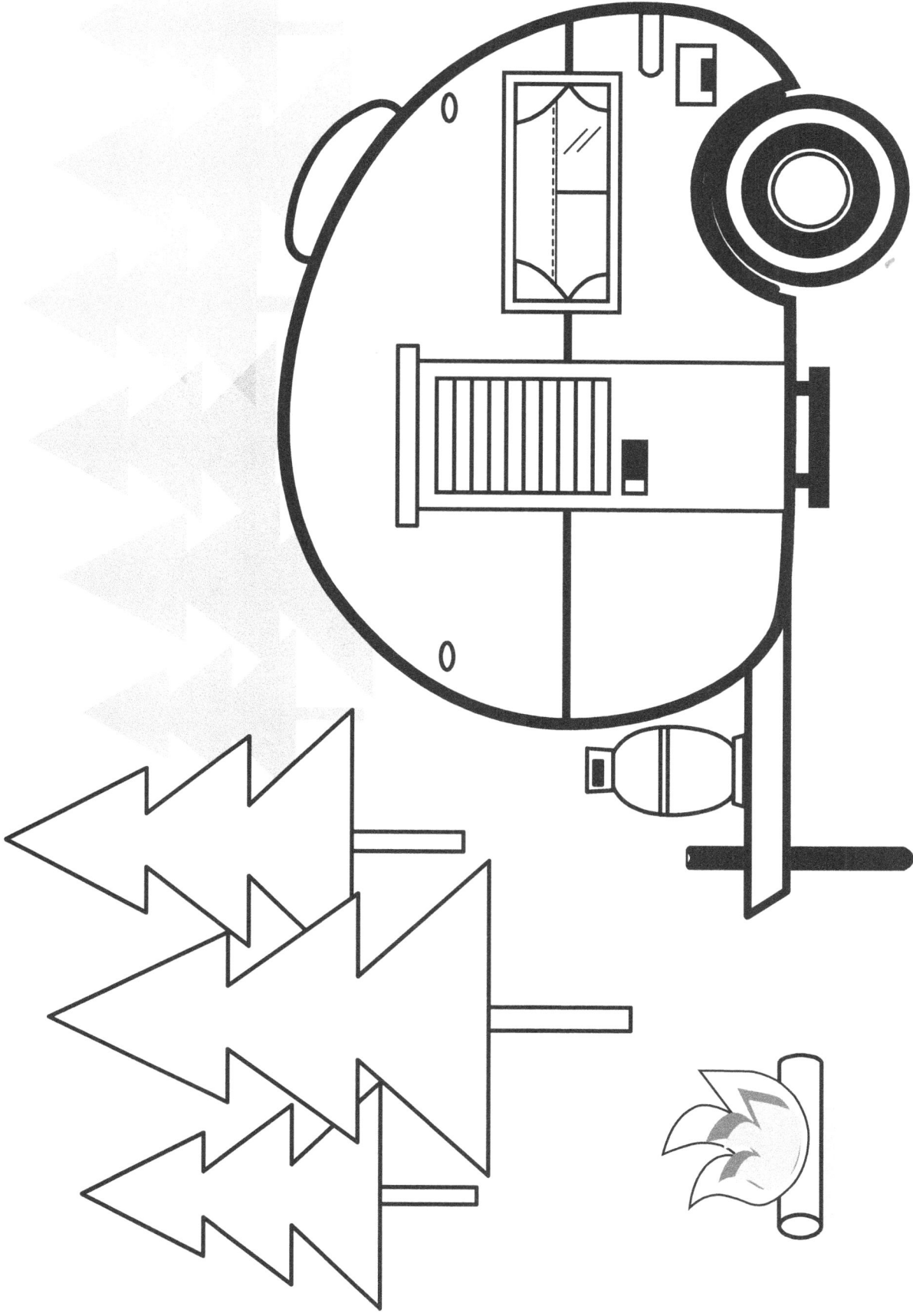

Let's Go CAMPING!

The Earth shows God's handiwork. Psalm 19:1

I am SO Loved!

John 3:16

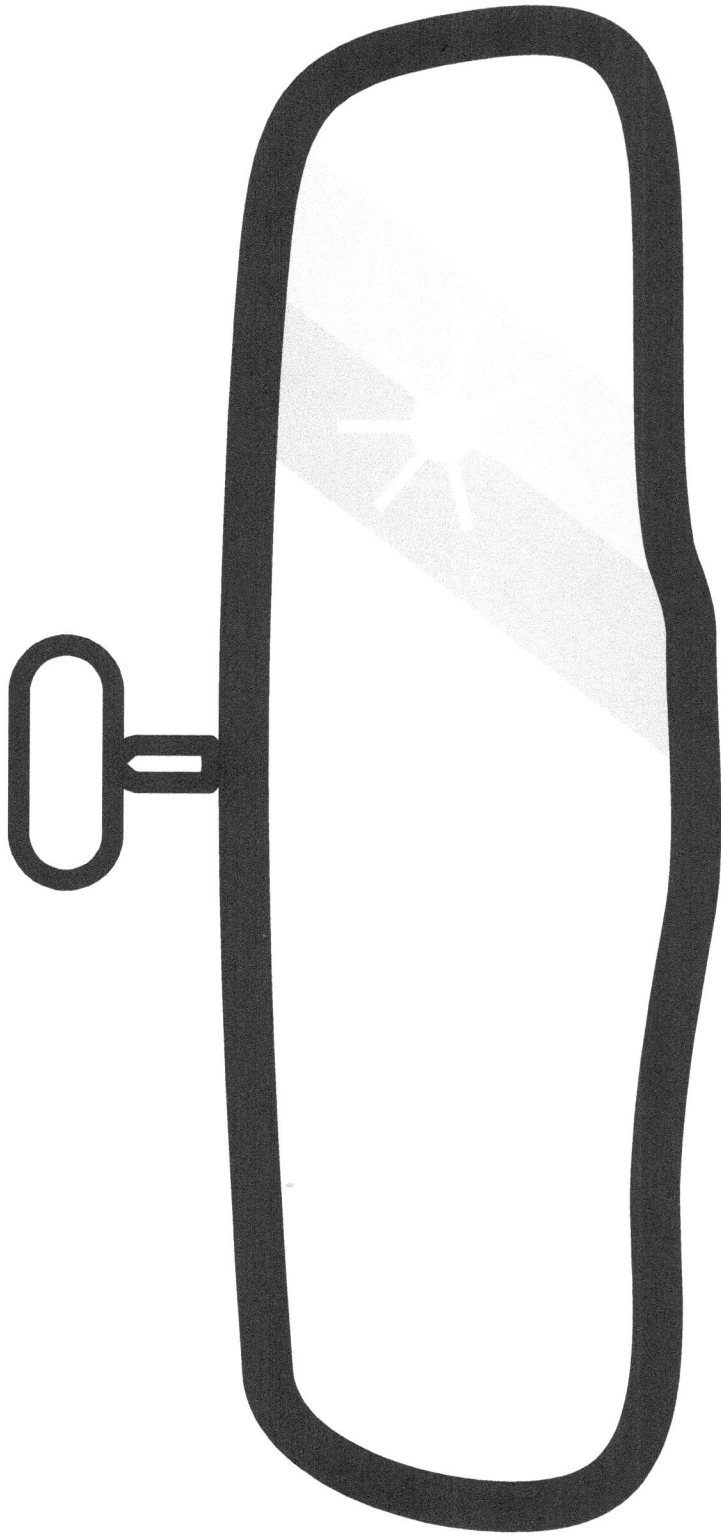

Leave It In The Rear View Mirror!

Sometimes a situation happens that you just want to forget. You are embarrassed or disappointed and need to move on. The Bible says, "Forgetting what is behind us, we look forward to what is ahead." Don't let a negative situation hold you back.

What needs to be in your past? Draw it in the rear view mirror.

My Paper Doll

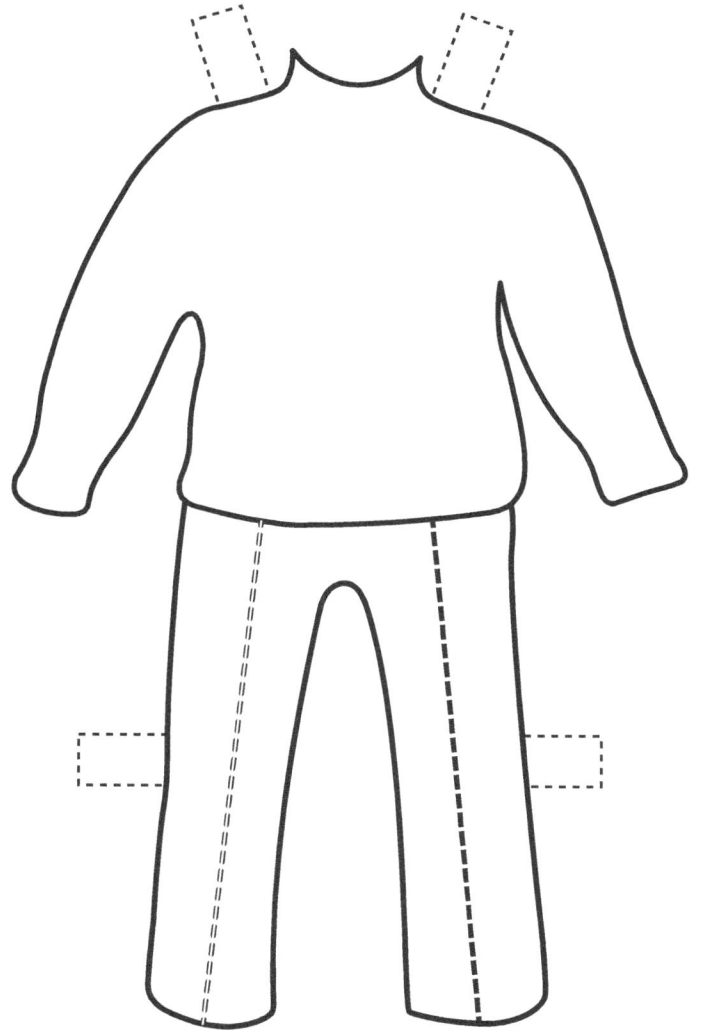

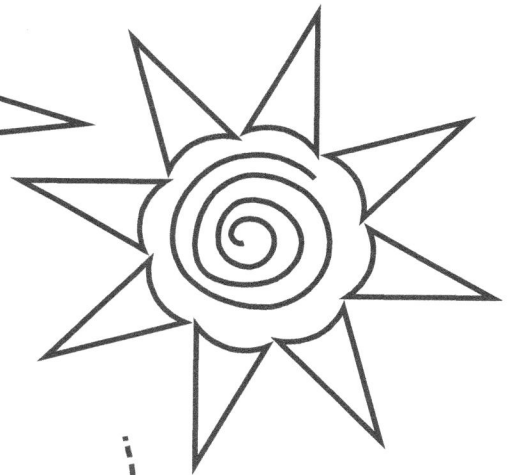

SUNSHINE
COMES IN
ALL FORMS

Create Your Own Sunshine:

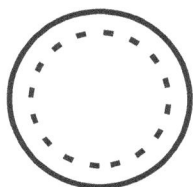

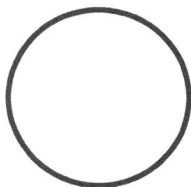

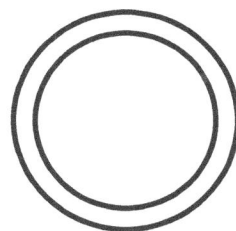

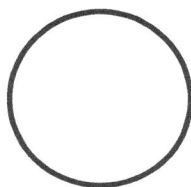

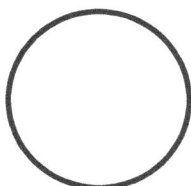

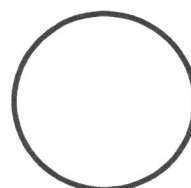

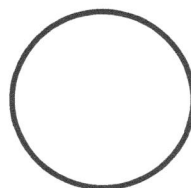

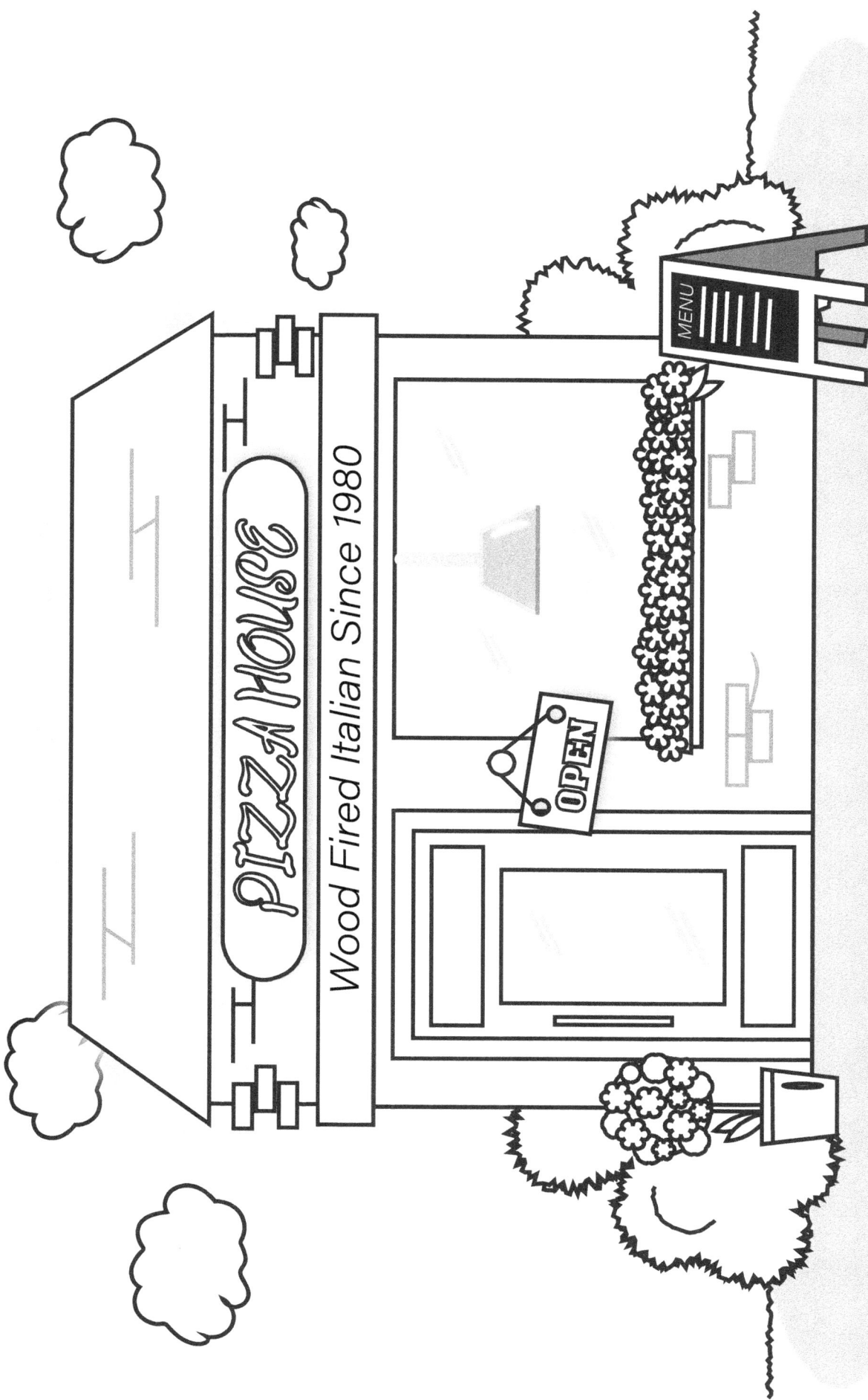

PIZZA HOUSE

Wood Fired Italian Since 1980

MENU

OPEN

I LOVE GOD MORE THAN PIZZA
AND I REALLY LOVE LOVE PIZZA!!!

Kids in the Kitchen

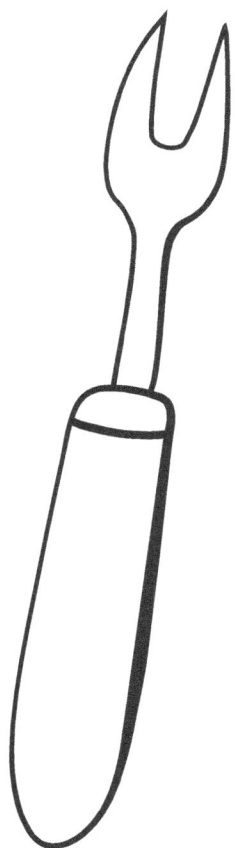

My BFF Is: ....

Having a best friend is important. We all need a friend we can trust and confide in; someone who supports us during the tough times and laughs with us during the good times.

Check the qualities below that you appreciate in your BFF:

○ MAKES ME SMILE AND LAUGH

○ IS ALWAYS GLAD TO SEE ME

○ HAS MY BACK WHEN I NEED THEIR SUPPORT

○ IS HONEST WITH ME, EVEN WHEN I DON'T AGREE

○ MAKES ME FEEL INCLUDED WITH OUR OTHER FRIENDS

○ ENCOURAGES ME ON THINGS I'M NOT AS GOOD AT DOING

○ LISTENS TO ME WHEN I'M TALKING

○ UNDERSTANDS WHEN I'M HAVING A BAD DAY

○ IS HAPPY FOR ME WHEN I HAVE A SUCCESS

○ _____

○ _____

I LOVE YOU

ALWAYS

and Forever

Create your own city street.
Put the names of your favorite
stores on the signs above
the buildings. Draw a stop sign at
the end of the street.

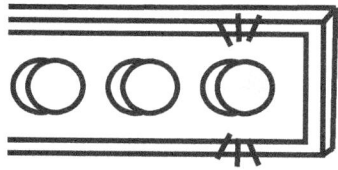

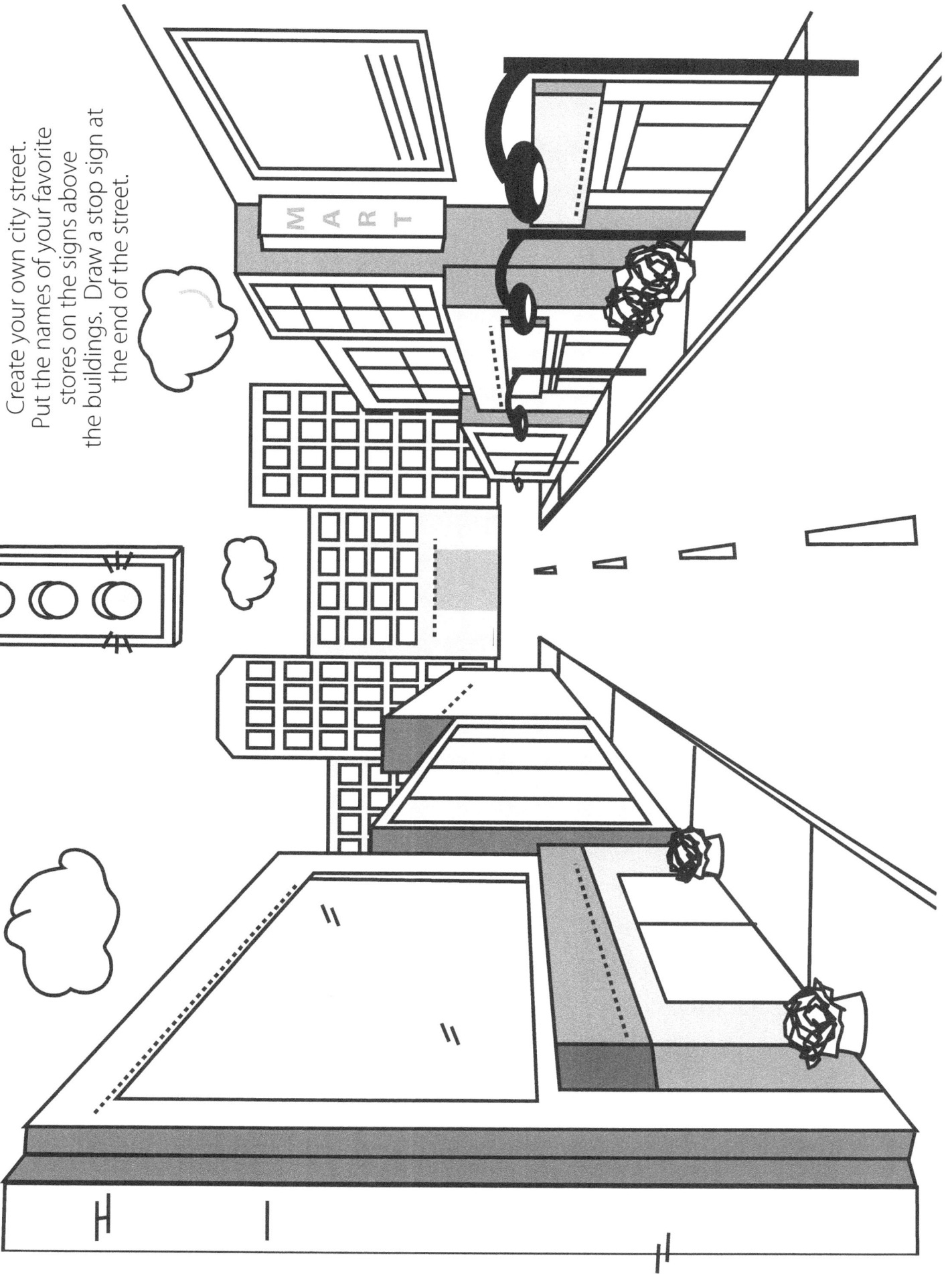

How Sweet Are Your Words to Me, Oh, Oh, Lord!

LISTEN UP!

My Voice Will Guide You

LIKE BEAUTIFUL SNOWFLAKES
YOU ARE ONE OF A KIND.

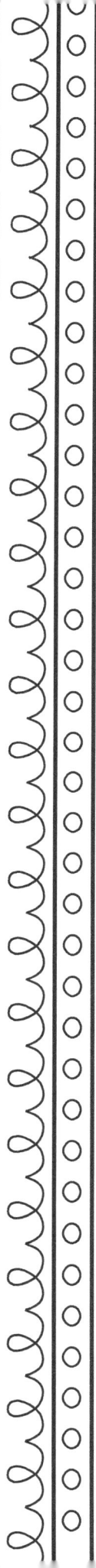

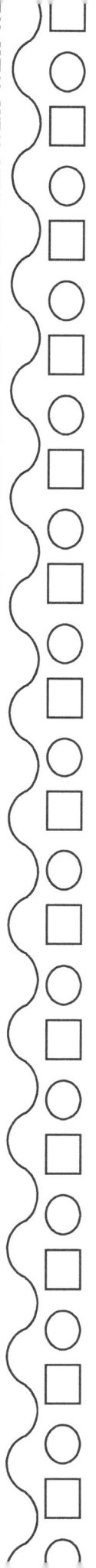

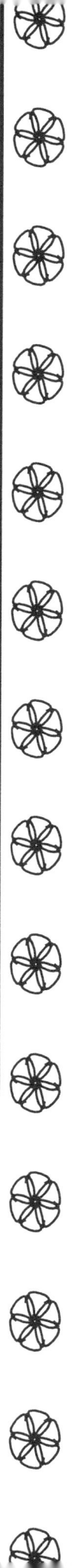

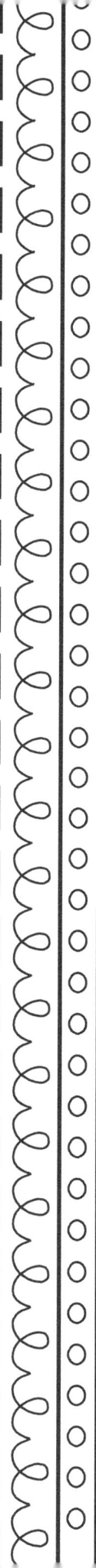

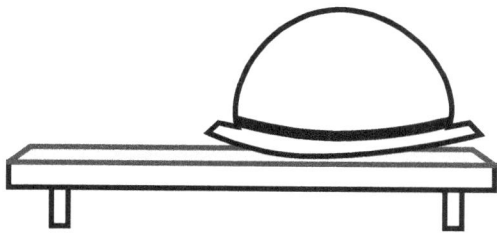

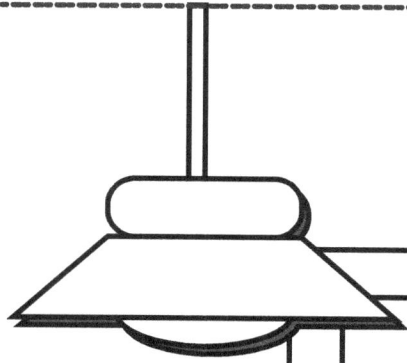

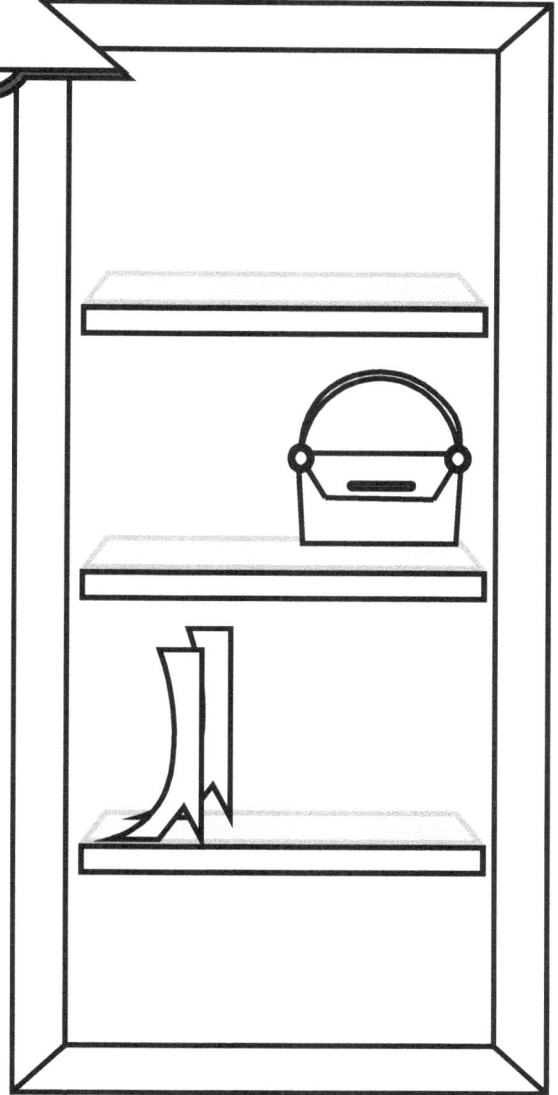

Draw some fun accessories to fill her closet.

Follow your HEART

But take your brain with you.

Alfred Adler.

JESUS LOVES ME

This I Know

Do you know the Lord loves you BIG TIME?
List ways Jesus shows His love to Y-O-U:

....

....

....

....

....

....

....

....

Got Goals?

I'll help you accomplish them.

— God

THE LORD IS MY STRENGTH AND MY SONG! EXODUS 15:2

See, I am sending an angel before you to protect you on your journey and lead you safely to the place I have prepared for you! Exodus 23:20

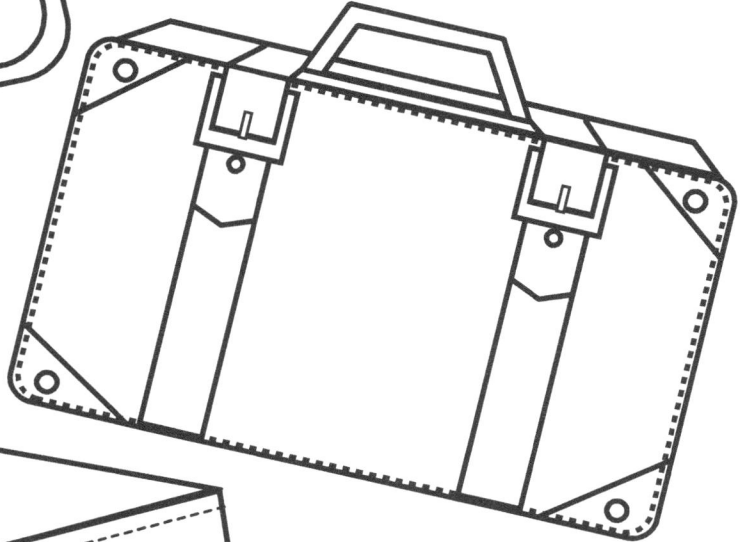

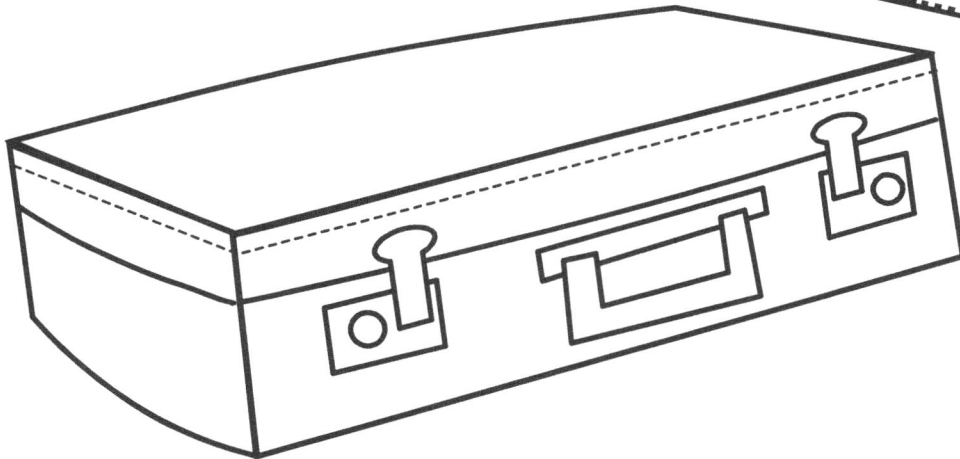

ANGELS WATCHING OVER ME!

I'M GOING PLACES!

Meet Your New Puppy! Choose a dog below. Add a name to its tag and decorate its collar.

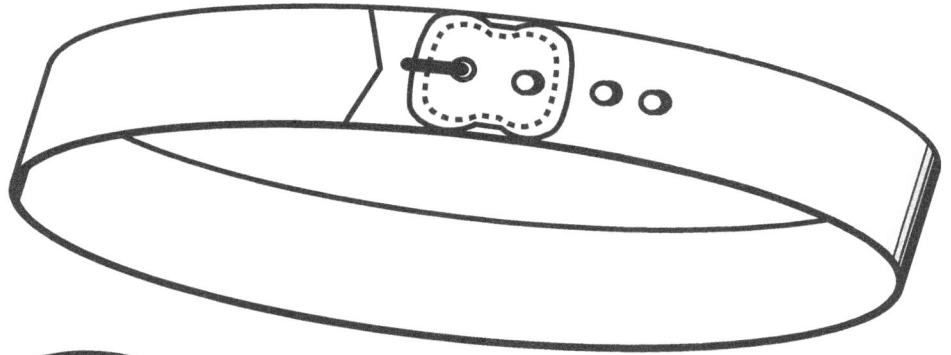

MY NAME IS
_____

I threw a party the day you were born.
Love You, God

WORLD'S BEST
CUPCAKES

BAKERY

Decorate the cupcakes below for your own special BAKERY. Don't forget the sprinkles!

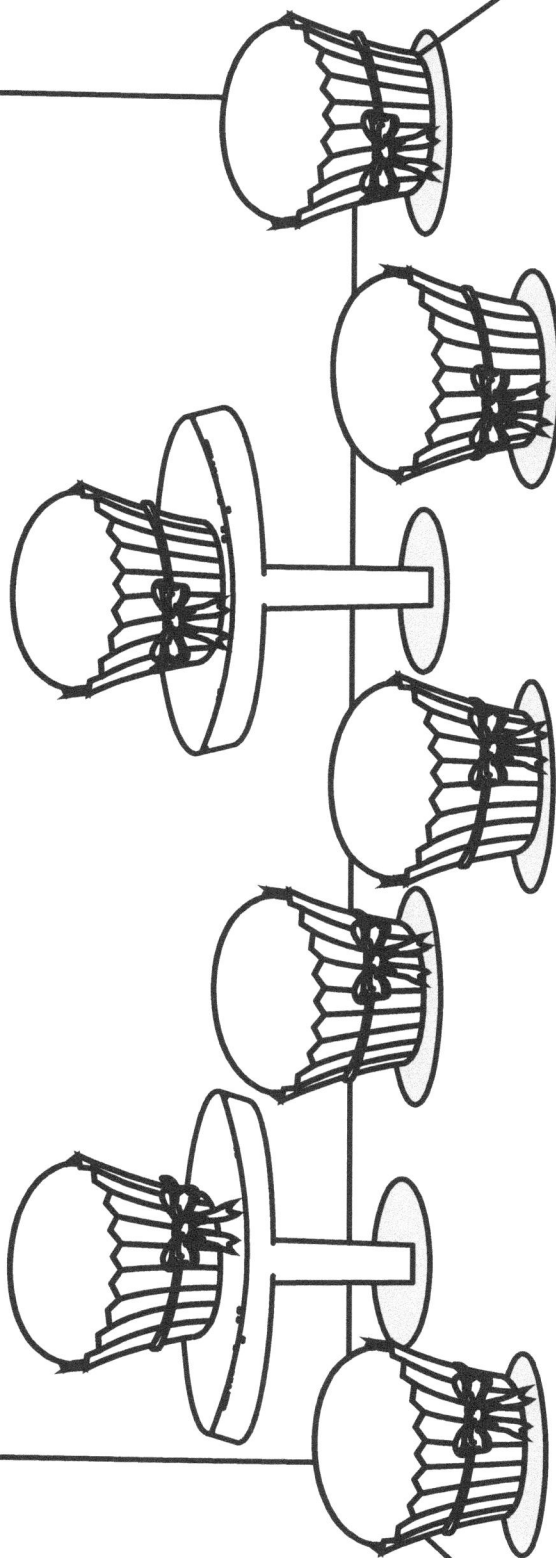

HOW ARE YOU FEELING?

We have different moods from day to day.
Review the faces below, then use the blank face
to draw how you feel right now.

HAPPY

ANGRY

SNEAKY

DISAPPOINTED

SURPRISED

SCARED

PEACEFUL

BORED

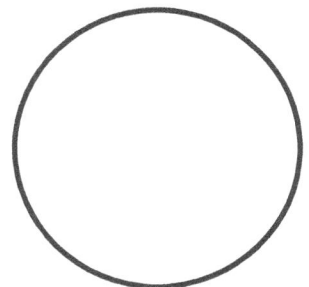

If It's IMPORTANT To YOU It's IMPORTANT To ME

-God

Just keep swimming!

YOU are an ORIGINAL

EVERY DAY IS A GIFT FROM GOD!

Decorate each special box below.

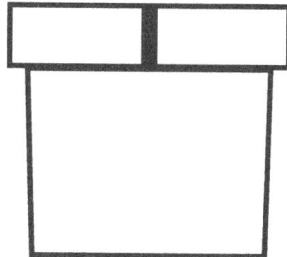

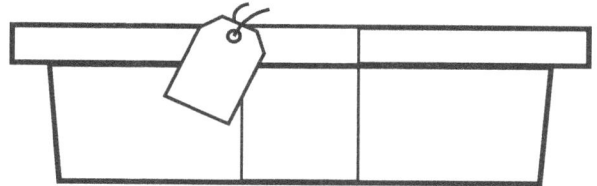

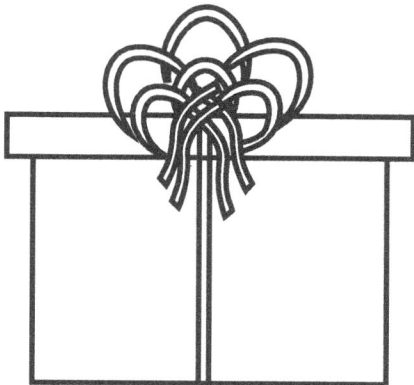

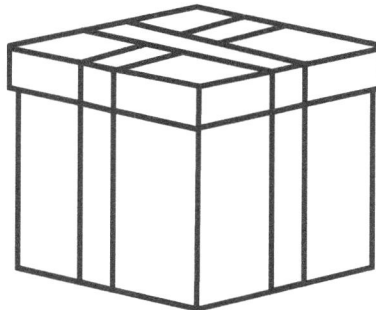

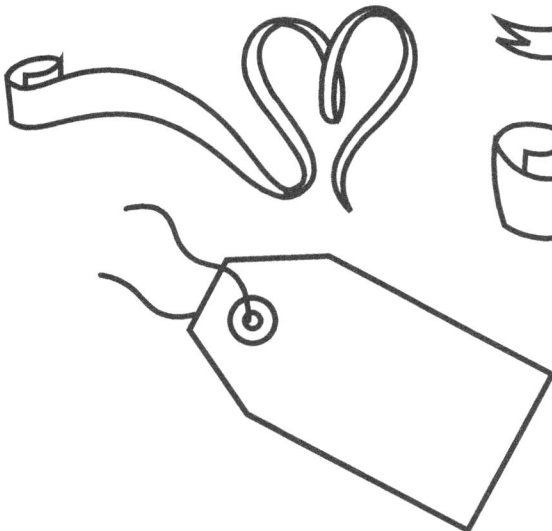

Don't forget to include: Tags, Curly Ribbons & Decorative Paper!

Be cool!

Love Jesus

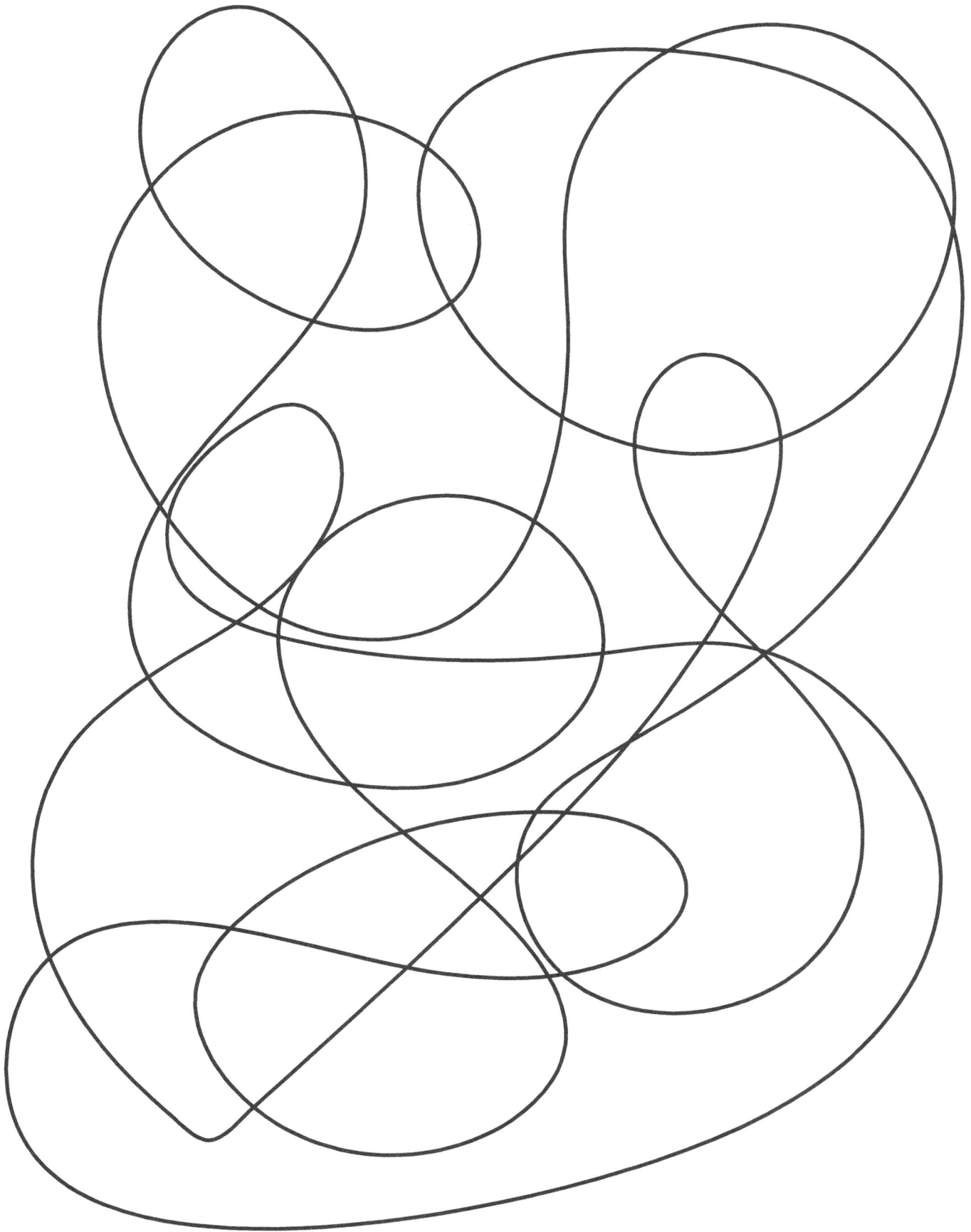

God makes all things beautiful. Even when we mess something up!
Put different colors and patterns in each individual section
and see how beautiful this design becomes.

Time to Design Your Own
THROW PILLOWS

Add fringe, cord, or
a pattern to decorate

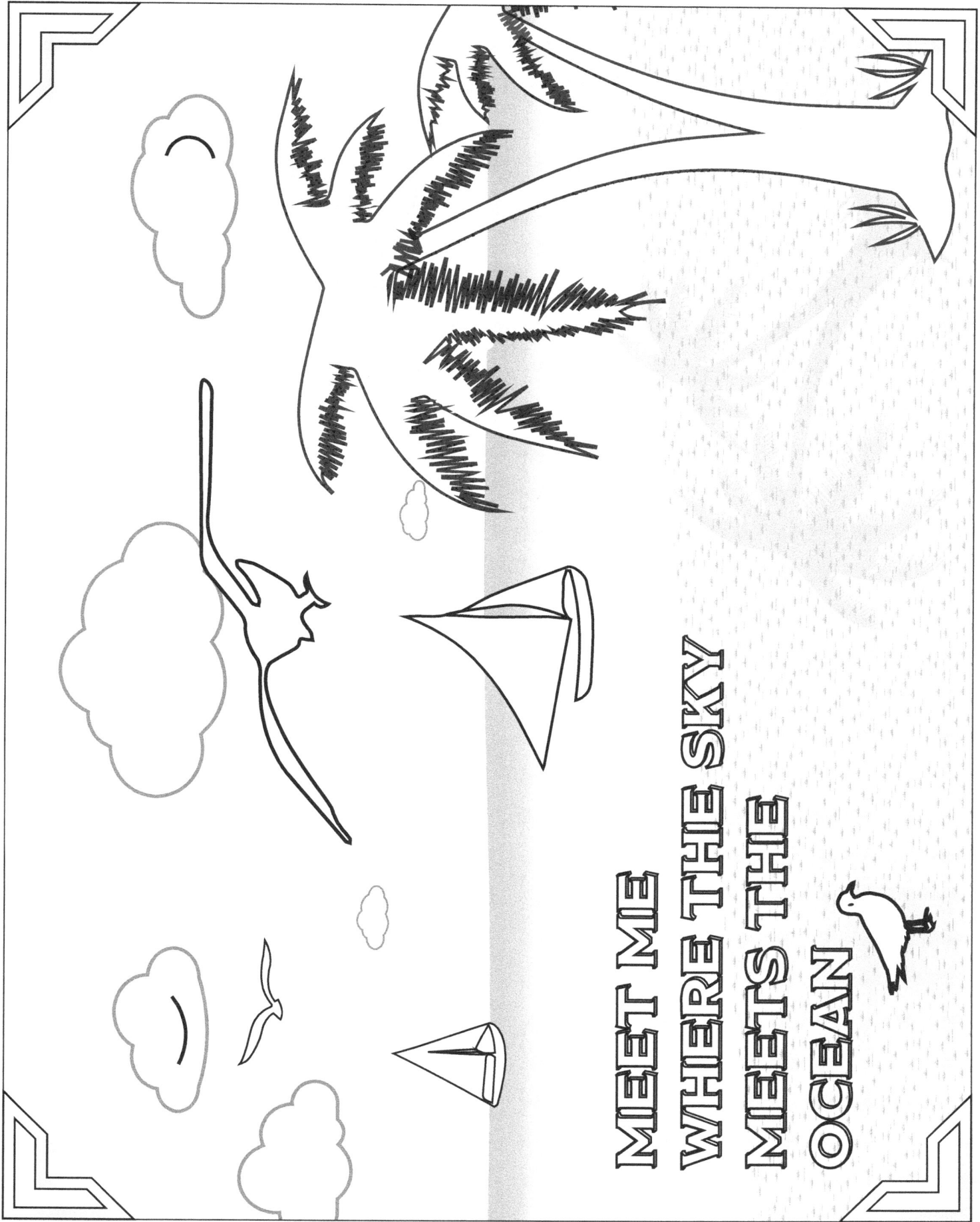

MEET ME
WHERE THE SKY
MEETS THE
OCEAN

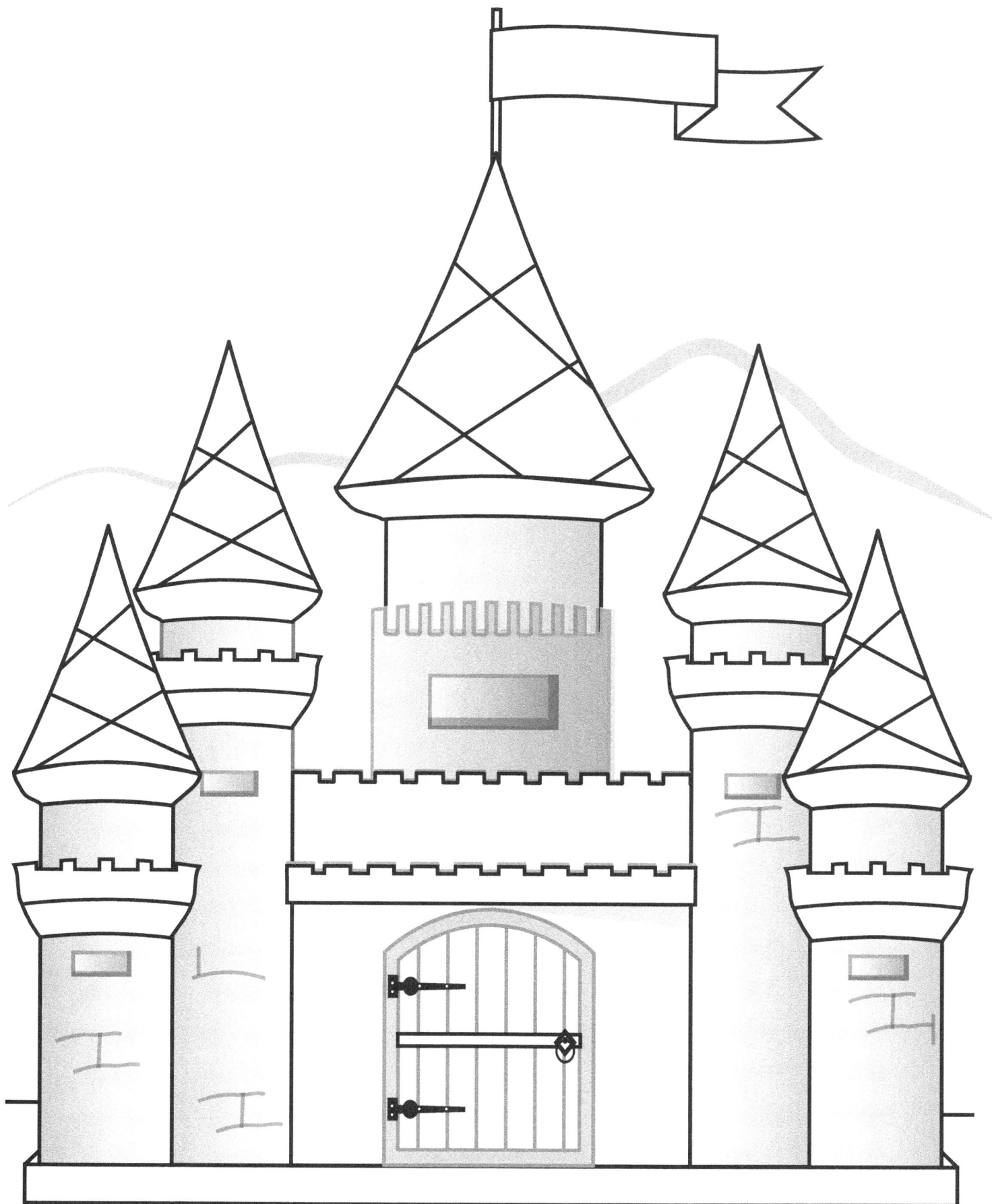

God is my bedrock under my feet, the castle in which I live,
my rescuing knight.   Psalm 18:2

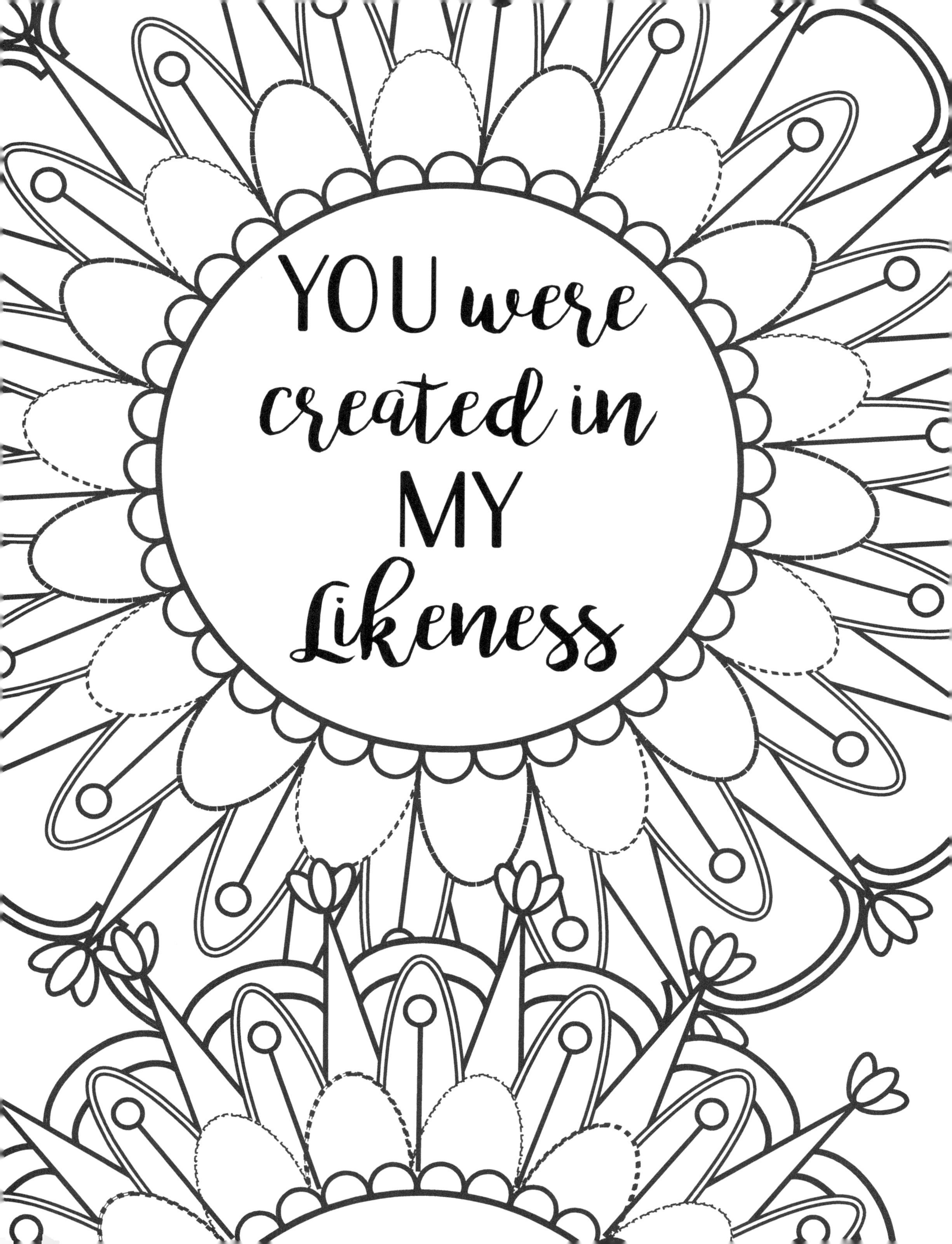
YOU were
created in
MY
Likeness

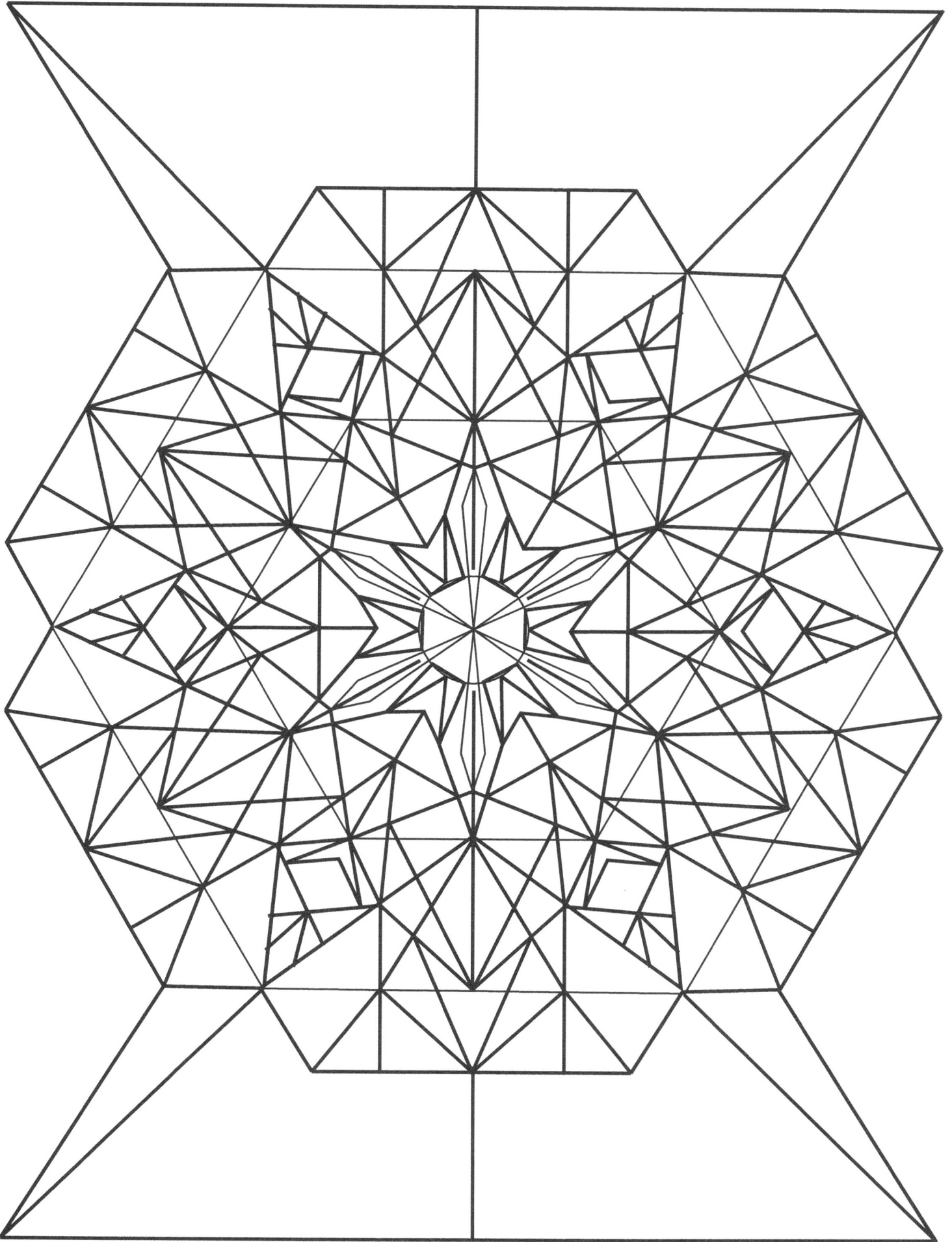

God made all creatures - big and small. Trace the dotted lines to uncover the animal below. Can you guess what it is? Color and detail the picture!

Teach me Your ways, O Lord.

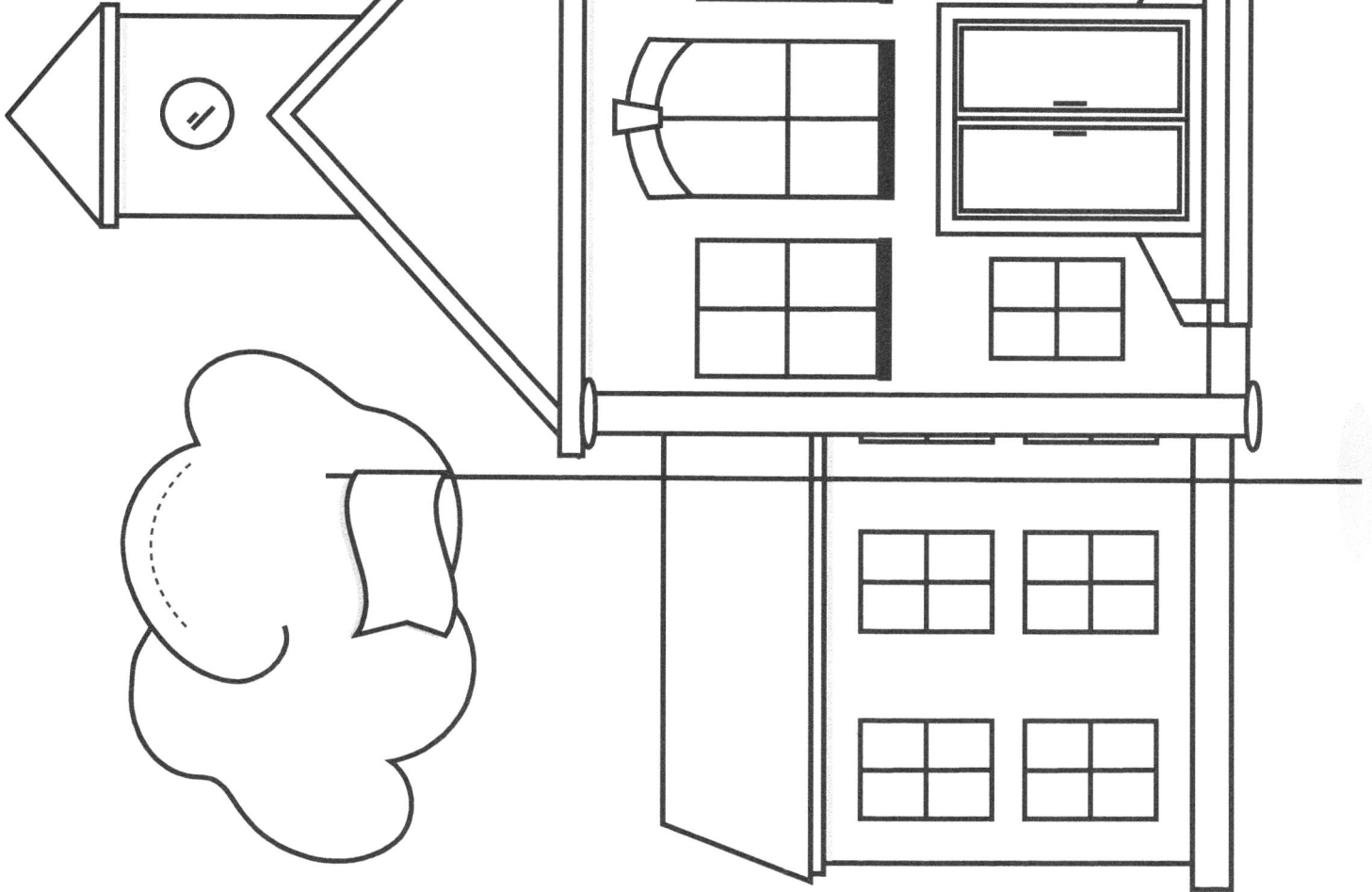

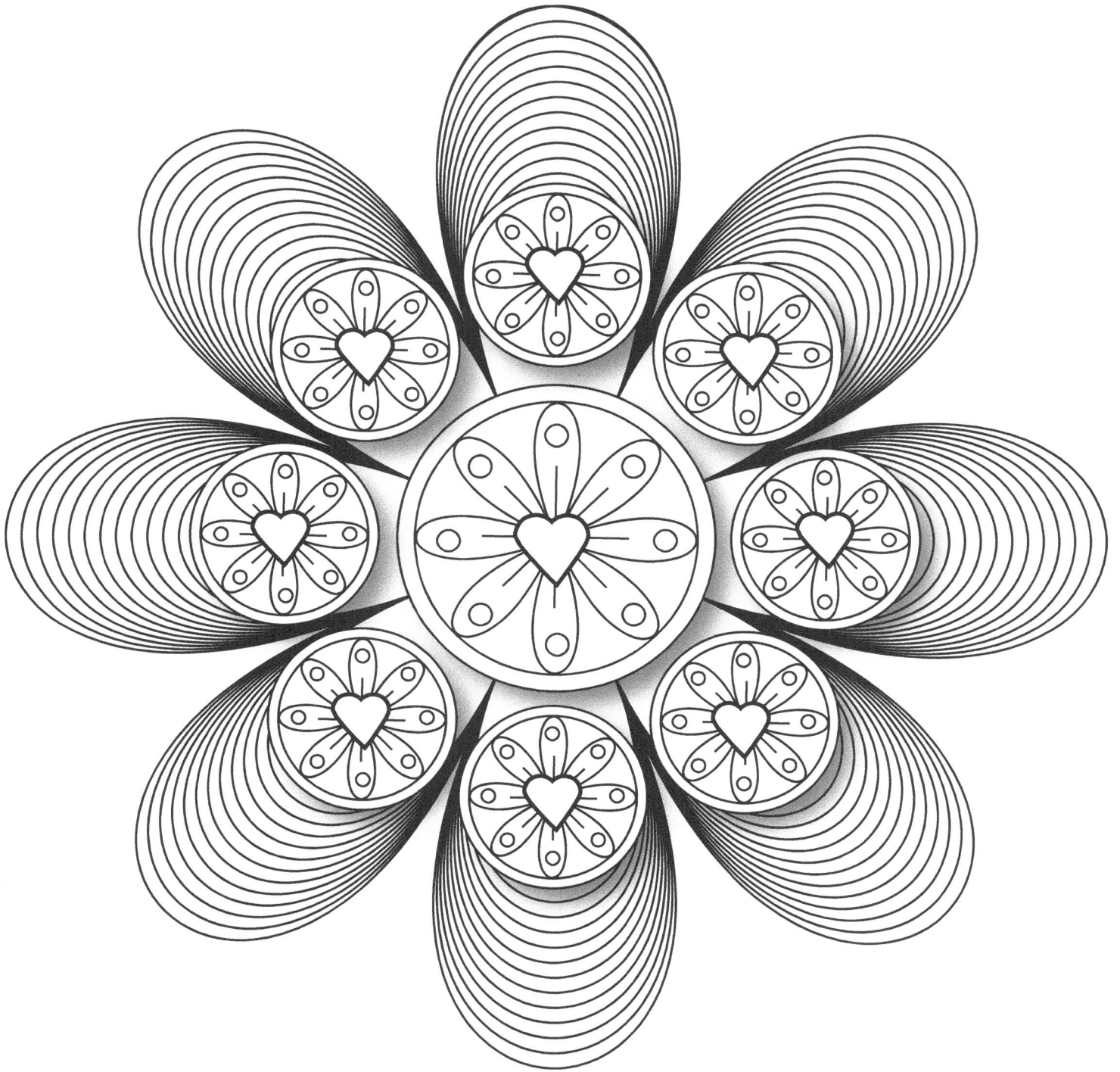

We Love Because
God First Loved Us.

www.ingramcontent.com/pod-product-compliance
Lightning Source LLC
Chambersburg PA
CBHW081147040426

42445CB)0015B/1790